Interactive Press

Café Boogie

Jenni Nixon trained at The Independent Theatre and worked as an actor for many years. She toured with the Queensland Theatre Company delivering classic and contemporary plays along with a poetry program.

As a performance poet Jenni has read at a wide range of events in Sydney, Melbourne, Wollongong and the Blue Mountains.

Her poem "visitor at home" won the 2002 Leonard Teale Memorial Prize at the Henry Lawson Festival, Gulgong, NSW.

Café Boogie was Commended in the IP Picks 2003 competition for unpublished poetry manuscripts.

Jenni lives in Sydney and is an active poet/performer at diverse venues.

The Emerging Authors Series showcases the best emerging Australian literary talent and is available in digital and print form.

Café Boogie

Jenni Nixon

Interactive Press
Brisbane

Interactive Press
an imprint of Interactive Publications
Treetop Studio • 9 Kuhler Court
Carindale, Queensland, Australia 4152
sales@ipoz.biz
www.ipoz/IP/IP.htm

First published by Interactive Press, 2004
© Jenni Nixon, 2004

Printed in 11 pt Book Antiqua on 14 pt Myriad Pro by QUT Printing and GOPRINT, Queensland, Australia. Made, printed and bound in Australia.

National Library of Australia
Cataloguing-in-Publication data:

Nixon, Jenni 1946 -
Café boogie.

ISBN 1 876819 20 0.

I. Title. (Series: Emerging authors)

A821.4

This project has been assisted by the Commonwealth Government through the Australia Council, its arts funding and advisory body.

that it will never come again is what makes life so sweet
– emily dickinson

words like swordfish through rain a kind of essential salvage
– vicki viidikas

Jacket design by David Reiter of Interactive Publications

Cover artwork: Michael Kelly, *café boogie*, 22cm x 30 cm
oil on canvas

Photos: Tracey Beckler

Acknowledgements are due to the following publications
where some of these poems first appeared sometimes in
different forms: *Cargo, Scant, Campaign, Sappho's Dreams
& Delights, Wild About the Roof, Illness, Overland, Overland
eXpress, Southerly, from the anabranch, Open Boat, Barbed Wire
Sky, five bells, Blue Dog, PixelPapers 24.*

"elsewhere in the city" lyrics: Bob Hudson's "Girls in Our
Town", sung by Margaret RoadKnight, © 1993, NewMarket
Music.

Acknowledgement is also due to artists involved in the
Moving Art Project.

Many people helped but special thanks to: georgina abrahams,
joanne burns, carolyn gerrish, kerry leves, alison lyssa, don
maynard, vera newsom, jenni paull, and dr david reiter.

My thanks to the women who over many cuppas provided
inspiration and encouragement.

Contents

Café Boogie

1. family

you've got fat
my mother's sly look
mouth a bitter pout
hunched stony
mind   a muddy swamp

you staying long?
counting coins
poverty is a poor relation
in second-hand clothes

we won't talk about it now
words as excess baggage
no books on <u>her</u> shelves
to offer sanctuary
allow escape

don't worry about me   I'm alright
brother yells   mother sulks
my legs shake

2. club

my brother takes me to the club to show me a good time

club fills with men beers smoke and women
   'free tea'   (at twenty bucks a cup)

chooks cross the road   gold miners dance
tigers roar   treasure chests open
girls become orchids

pavlov dogs with musical losses
you play big to win big
keep changing the bet
(confuse the computer)
change machines often
play the same one
keep money in
take money out
women wave hands like wands

my brother loses a week's wages
next night   we go again

3. *town*

strained smiles   my mother waves
in a month   she will be dead

Eddy Avenue   stench of garbage   people
along Parramatta Road   *go get 'em*   towers
sunset reflections   pretty pink windows of opportunity

home   thirsty garden's weeds   car alarm wails a protest
water bombed kids screech   TVs prattle at each other
gossip   two young dads   dead of overdose   *two of 'em*
smack is always so pure at Christmas

go again to a club   at blackjack machine
pretty blonde   not drinking   teaches me how to play
suddenly game's too fast   lines of cocaine in the loo
I leave *lady luck*   the illusion of company
go back to the slots   make up for loss   with more loss

my mother is dying   her legs are black
I hear her fear   down the phone   from the hospital
nothing I can do   protected by distance
tell her it'll be okay   when I arrive   she is dead
she wanted me to tell her story   but
hard enough to find words of my own

hers are scribbled on clumps of torn up paper
slurred speech   drugs and shock therapy
sighs   and long silences   mood swings
stories of giving up   inconsolable
teasing sexual revelations   in men's clothing
picking up strangers   Lifeline and the Methodists

my father beat her   took her hostage
controlled the drugs   demanding surrender
as a kid   she lived in fear   of headless ghosts in England
at eighteen   of shock therapy   (without anaesthetic)
put away in psych hospitals   then in an early marriage
hopes of her   *settling down*   failing

I am a seagull   No   No   I am an actress
played the Independent Theatre and the Theatre Royal
studied Art at the Julian Ashton School   painting on cloth
canvas   ceramics: magical horses   flowers
in a pottery factory   employing Germans after the war
making pots and painting them   kilns   paint and glue
copied aboriginal designs   *mimi*   stick figures   kangaroo
little Dutch boy and girl salt and pepper shakers

anything was appropriated   small white round plastic frames
held dried wildflowers from Western Australia

prints of The Blue Boy   or a Flemish master with plumed hat
sold to David Jones and Farmers   I 'd go with her
to Rowe Street picture framers for supplies
till the business went broke   Japanese flooded the market
cheap copies for tourists

a scandal followed   door to door sellers
in Canberra   mentioned in Parliament
Dad in gaol for tax fraud   Mum in an asylum
both parents locked away   I escape to fantasy
fast canoe rides down rocky river curves
without any paddles

    * * *

a few good frocks   most are stained   receipts from 1976
cracked glaze on the pottery she made   old *Readers' Digests*
exercise books of jokes she'd copied out by hand

at the casket   hands raised   minister prays   *let go*
anger guilt regret   she's in God's hands   neighbours say
you look so much like her   she never had a harsh word

I walk through rooms   abandoned   numb
play Sinead O'Connor's *faith and courage*
cling to a Scarpetta crime book on cutting up corpses

    * * *

at the memorial club in the rose garden
her ashes with my father's spread
my brother chose the plaque: *reunited at last*

on the toilet reading   a book on pilots and planes   *Final Flight*
his heart stopped   a swift departure   my father had his album
from the air force in New Guinea filled with photos of planes
and native women planes and naked breasts and him too young
filling up parachute spaces with scotch to sell to yankees for profit
he crashed once in the jungle was lost for days in humid heat
I remember scrubbing his broad back   again and again
making it red and hot and sudsy smooth   a big man
he spread his real estate salesman self about all over the flat plains
in five different patterns Cape Cod and others   scattered seed too
with the neighbour's wife and girls he could get wherever possible
did patterns sprout up in other families?   he retired back
to his country of graziers   the sea and clubs
Les Murray landscape   dry heat-shimmer roads
through paddocks at the back of the Gloucester Buckets
happier with his sisters   and in his bowling whites
beer in hand   new car in the garage   at Christmas
he wouldn't take out   *those Mexicans*
from down south there   too many of 'em   are maniacs
can't bloody drive   so he stayed inside till they left
we sang hymns and red poppies were placed upon his coffin
as his mates claimed him   he always was theirs anyway
a visitor at home   brawling with mum   waiting
to go back to the club   be with men   who understood   the way of wars

grandfather sent postcards from Gallipoli   mostly sepia
*L*ANDING *1915   D*UG *O*UTS *AT *G*ABA *T*EPE   *T*HE *P*YRAMIDS *AND *S*PHINX*
he'd joined the Australian Imperial Expeditionary Force at 19

*A*RMY *S*ERVICE *C*ORPS *AT *G*ALLIPOLI* **1915**

*Here is a good view of Anzac Cove   You can see timber carts to carry shells
and water in khaki kerosene tins   The beach used to be shelled
from right to left but is not so bad since advance to Lonesome Pine
Near the stores on the left   a shell gave me my baptism of fire   landed 4ft away*

Lonesome Pine not Lone Pine   Freudian slip
or was it a big-sky mountain   on the *Trail of the Lonesome Pine*
Zane Grey shootout adventure?

*C*HURCH *AT *L*EMNOS* **1915**

*This Greek church looks like a "white elephant"   the only building in Lemnos
worth looking at   I walked around by the stone wall on the left   near the trees
spent 11 days here   before going to Heliphatio Hospital with ear trouble*

*G*UEZIREH *R*ED *C*ROSS *H*OSPITAL *– *C*AIRO*

*A beautiful building has delicate iron work on the balconies
a group of officers and chaps in slouch hats pose outside*

*M*EMORY *OF *A*USTRALIANS *AT *A*NZAC* **1915**

scattered graves dug where soldiers fell
mounds of soil   some with rocks and a wooden cross
(no message scribbled on the back)

kept souvenirs from the war   his watch that took a direct hit to the face
buckled inwards in the shape of a bullet and a Turkish metal arrow
remembers until the end of his life   whistling shells
ringing in his ears (tinnitus)   England in 1920 met Gran and married
has two daughters   a business   down among market gardens
on Sydney's northern shore selling native seed   tiny
feather light   or shiny black and hard   rows of bottles
stamps that came in return   corners torn off packages in faded colours
zebras giraffes   gazelles from South Africa   all to be soaked and sorted

memories of him driving on the wrong side of the road
in his yellow FJ Holden   searching maturing seed pods
calculating when ready to collect   with Izzy
who ran with a wheelbarrow   never walked   chattering in Arabic
cleaning seed together   some that fell through   growing weirdly tall
under the house in dug out earth   hessian bags
filled with seed pods and cones   I'd sit there with a hammer
smashing open macadamia nuts   gobbling handfuls
of creamy nut squashed on the brick

Grandpa took me to see a new invention in the hardware store window
black and white flickering images   later we saw Betty Cuthbert win
at the Melbourne Olympics   packed into small envelopes
he counted fine seed at a cost of three or four pence
never said what he thought when I used the Gallipoli postcards
on stage in Tennessee Williams' *Camino Royale*
"dirty postcards   dirty postcards"
Gran made me an apron to carry them   an extra in the crowd
with more *business* than the lead actress
"pretty postcards   pretty postcards"

when he won the Kings cup for rifle shooting   he looked embarrassed
in *The Melbourne Herald*   carried through the streets   as men cheered
he rarely talked about the war   never marched on Anzac Day
never met with old cronies for a drink   or wore his medals on display
each morning with breakfast   would read the *Herald*
carefully peel an apple   examining the obituaries

afraid to see his name appear   he published a small book of poems
love and soldiers' dreams   weeding and rabbits' habits
believed the Book of Revelation's Armageddon   imminent

left me with the legacy of a green thumb
love of roses   flowering natives
when out walking
a habit of collecting seed   dried to grow another day
making notes in a journal:
'*this species is a common shrub*'
tasting words on the tongue   '*hippeastrum*'
germinating words into poems

this year the spathiphyllum (peace) lily flowered only once
gift from a friend who died from AIDS
children scream with delight in Elkington Park
a rusty sea gull cleans feathers stained in an oil spill
fruit bats fight for figs from the Moreton Bay

a local man all in black   on board the 442
as it weaves   down hilly roads   round tight corners
into narrow leafy streets   past cluttered workers' cottages
and million dollar town houses   plots and plans
secession for Balmain   an end to libraries
he writes methodically in his little black book
a useless waste of the public purse
the poor can have their words delivered in a van

at the local hospital fete   a skeleton stands guard
a nurse makes plaster casts on kids' arms for fun
in Sarajevo they've stopped shooting housewives
men talk of peace and plant trees

which of my neighbours
would snipers have shot today?

number 82176 is two
no toys

adults make kites
coloured rubbish bags
guards confiscate them
number 82176 is in tears

plays   with garbage
wailing   waddling
little hands waving

ahead of U. N. inspection
detainees are to be referred to
by name   not number
have their rooms repainted
trees planted
razor wire removed

red dust swirls
heat   no fans
Fatimah (number 82176) stays
locked away

a young man   off his medication   set his flat alight
taken away to hospital   he's charged with endangering lives
sent to prison   five days   a young woman screams
anguished bellowing   rattling around in her flat   or
prowling the grounds   screams   *I'm 25 years old*
why can't you leave me alone   as she breaks a window
smashes her possessions   screams   *leave me alone*
what have I done to you?   an Iraqi man   painting
Dept of Housing window-frames pink   green or brown
(look less institutional not like hospital white)   asks
where is her mother   her brother   a young girl like that
where is her family to take care of her?   rumours circulate
gang-raped by Stephen and his mates   worst case of schizophrenia
unmanageable   catches taxis she can't pay
cadges fare on buses   (says she lost her wallet)
a Bette Davis chronic smoker   bludging smokes
constantly yelling paranoia   neighbours feel stalked
afraid to come home   they increase their medication
speak with the tenancy client manager   who says
ring the police   crisis team   police   come and go
she escapes   the crisis team is no longer handling her case
Dept of Housing is cancelling her lease:
failure to live up to the conditions of the bond   a month later
her things are thrown from the windows
taken away to the tip by contractors

when she took another lover
we blamed each other
sought freedom in selective amnesia
on a visit   we're strangers
silence grows   as years pass
I still think of her
what might have been
plans made and not kept
our future together
I wouldn't be so alone
were she here   to betray again

evidence

we now have evidence that we are not important
– Stephen Hawking

stuck in a black hole
within a universe of 100 billion trillion stars
as many grains of sand as there are
on this lonely planet

stories seen   on our own screens
are projections – seductions / fears
adapted fantasies
from an unreliable witness

living alone   without progeny
no maternity leave / childcare benefits
no family tax cuts
for you

the sound of a found poem
we apologise for the delay
your call is important to us
so please continue to hold…

then music – Mozart's *Divertimento*
'Out of this world'   I mutter
to no one / to a recording
we apologise for the delay

in the darkness   listening to rain
breathe deeply   slowly

acceptance may come

you can still hear the song   faintly off key
I love the nightlife   I love to boogie
through grey smoke   as gossipy men drink coffee
squashed into the Piccolo Bar   up The Cross
smell of hashish lingers like joints that come too slow
you want to belong   be another 'identity'
stuck on the walls   fading photos
of Show people   staying young forever

shadows appear   late at night
Butch in his corner   near the door
easy to see customers   or   make an escape
takes from a stash in his wooden leg
the best   acid   speed   and hashish
before the good times ended
in Long Bay   with a loss of privileges
I met Butch years later on a bus in Oxford Street
Ten years since last I smoked green leaf   I said
Ten minutes   looking at his watch
Yeah   ten minutes it'd be   for me.

I can see them   old friends
sitting in the empty café seats
where strangers enjoy strong coffee
and talk of football and the David Jones sale
a coin drops in the juke box
I love the nightlife   I love to boogie
brassy beat   doesn't disturb
all those frozen smiles

a pack of women and kids   in the beer garden of a pub
The Bald Something   Stag or Rock   down by White Bay
lost in a back street   littered with graffiti
where cargo vessels unpack bankrupt luxuries
oil sits on water   waiting the tide out
I'm steamed alive   lobster pink
menopausal flush rises from chest to throat
soggy with sweat   a barren wetness:
strange place for a baby shower

the women are my neighbours and friends
the daughter   big belly blown up balloon
children play Nintendo / Pokemon   or run at hide & seek
footballers sing loudly *I'm just crazy about the way we move*
                    doing the Eagle Rock
their voices rise   surprising   lovely base notes
lovers hold hands   exchange hurried kisses
beer slops over middy glasses
as mates prop up the bar   pokies chirp musical loss

top sorts at this table   do you mind if I sit down?
red curls frame freshface   in clean white shirt and neat jeans
pulls up a chair to talk   of tug boats   and throwing a line
we take tons of used soil from Manly sewage   across the harbour
for reprocessing as landfill   up Parramatta   smell's so bad
it burns off the nose hair you got growing   it's that strong
shit of a job   I'm blushing rose pink   *this your first baby shower?*
yeah you bet   looks eagerly down the table   *top sorts and no men.....*

we come here often   she says   opening gifts
blankets   toys   little baby clothes   *the food's great*
outside harbour grease

washes up against wooden planks
squeaking with the swell
container cranes hover over crates
big birds with nests of square eggs
we wait for food   restless
thin women plan a boozy night
picking up blokes   smoke in the fuggy air

platters arrive   chunks of tasty cheese
topped with snippets of olive and gherkin   in a sea of Jatz
overcooked finger food   no salad
her mouth   a thin tight line drawn where her lips disappear
pleading with her mother her friends   talk to the kitchen staff
tell 'em it's not good enough   not worth thirty-five bucks a platter

in a pretend skirmish   the footballers tackle each other
shout encouragement   swilling beer
through smiles   Tugboat Johnny is blowing smoke rings
I exit   wiping sweat   as the noise level rises

a trunk of cheese massive load of supplies
gear piled into the back of a ute
to be flown out on a rickety plane
taking them to the ice

women joined together in a test of courage
on the Discovery Channel
haven't raised all the money for the trip
we're good on the ice not so good at fund raising

reaching for my tea is difficult
I'm frozen to the spot
the remote has disappeared
down a crevasse in the sofa

rugged up in snow gear   off on an adventure
flying over ice   for miles   and miles
to trudge   to the magnetic centre   the polar cap
frozen grey mountains   slippery weeks
slogging against the wind
we plan to parachute   on skis   to the North pole   itself

I cannot watch
some danger seen from the sofa
is intolerable

on an uneven playing field
sisters doing it for themselves

these are not my hands at the wheel   you've run the lights
we're moving too fast   headed toward a crash
you're ignoring all warning signals   plunged into traffic
we're going the wrong way   go back   no detours
try to keep to a map don't go down that road
discarded speeding tickets litter your trail
we're spinning out of control   Help
there's too much baggage on board   this is a Tow Away area
Clear way   Do not park   *give an inch they take a mile*
watch for a roundabout   don't let's go over old ground
you don't   Stop   Revive   Survive   you hurtle past
intent on the destination   what scenery?
we are passing collision sites where wreaths litter
you want every detail   past convictions   car ownership insurance
can we avoid   pot holes   road humps   obstructions
innocent bystanders   pedestrians   cops   courts   lawyers   animals
driving blind   down dusty roads highways   bi ways
lost   praying for a cul-de-sac

where did Lilith go after banishment?
was she an ecstatic   refusing to lie under Adam
world's first woman   manic depressive?
with so much joy in the Garden of Eden
falling into disarray   sinking down to a dark cavern
wreaking terrible revenge   snacking   on the heads of babies
or is this just another   Old Men's Tale   to frighten little children

prodded
squeezed
  squashed
      in ultrasound seek within
            vast cosmos   each breast
                  swirling seas   black orbs
                  cysts
            waiting to be discovered
        aspirated   sent for biopsy
grey movement
flows
  black holes
    appear
    vanish
    uneven rocks
  a lunar landscape
unfamiliar terrain
within soft curves
magnets of pleasure
after probe
joy to discover
upon exploration
nothing unusual to report

hot day   down Circular Quay   sitting on a harbour seat
licking gelato   admiring living statues   so skilled
at playing the crowd   Statue of Liberty   slim stillness
billowing skirt   holds up a flurry of stars   in seconds
a thief grabs money from performer's bowl   suddenly
the silvery Statue of Liberty   has the thief
by the throat   up against a wire wall   pleading
let me go   gruff male voice demands   *give it back*
what could be more shocking?   that the statue
isn't a young woman   or that muscles long held still
are so strong   move quickly   as the thief
hands back notes and runs off   statue screams
I'll get the cops   don't let me see you again
american tourists drop ten yankee dollars
give me your poor and downtrodden   Symbol of Freedom
lifts his grubby skirt   city grime has turned silver to grey
tucks into safety hard won wages   returns to posing
a youth on a skateboard cruising by   yells
Look out!   a plane's coming!

i call at twenty to twelve   for a piece of the charity cake
try to explain   had a fall   arm in plaster
walking stick helpless   pensioner   can't shop for Christmas

the woman's   too busy to listen

'there's a long wait   can you manage?'

before i reply   dulcet tones   ABC round vowels
voice beautiful   and Beethoven
interrupted every few minutes

our welfare lines are still busy   please hold the line

an hour and ten minutes

our welfare lines are still busy

continue to wait   how long?   perverse curiosity
invest my time in a Christmas hamper
sugary sweetness   tinned with nuts
or cancel the whole event   just another day

our welfare lines are still busy   please hold the line

painful reminder   poverty sucks
quarter past one

a hamper will arrive on the 20th

a minute passes   taking details
how many people   are out there
just holding on?

our welfare lines are still busy   please…

words   like
icicles
hang   there
pointed
painful
frozen
in the
air

conversational brawl

visit Manly   7 miles by ferry   1000 miles from care

I'm brushing sand from a ferry seat
thinking of Slessor's mate overboard
pewter clouds smother baby blue sky
two pelicans glide across the city
maxi yachts flirt with the wind
grand ferries perform ballroom dances
white petticoat waves   gracious turns in broad sweeps
cracked face floppy hat woman expertly weaves her boat
through choppy waters   under the coat hanger bridge

we paced corridors together   smoking grimly   ironies
on yellow walls in loony bins   familiar Van Gogh paintings
attended heartache auditions cattle call
drank   vivacious growing shrill

you cook in the bedroom   TV sound gone   fridge door's falling off
I'm uncomfortable   squirming in a broken chair
you want me to stay   hear your poems   I want sand and sea
come all this way to Manly   sunshine going with a southerly gale

mirror mirror on the wall   look at you   see me   rage at loss
what might have been   you replay scenes of betrayal
I can't stay to pick up the pieces   you bristling with blame
impatient with kindness   mock my choices
we leave lunch on the table   walk slowly to the sea
find wind whipped waves   too rough to swim

24

naked buttocks
exposed
by the pull of the tide

woman leans towards man
snuggles in   bares
brown perky breasts

small boy   giggles
at water's edge
yellow spade and tonka toy

wild surf
young boys on boogie boards
splash out to sea

escape from city madness
toes in sand   delight
sprinkles of rain   tickle my back

seconds in time   a sandy spot
beside spliced waves of volcanic rock
frozen millennia ago

currawongs fly above my pale body
rasp a warning
silky black squawking cries

black shadows   gone too fast
one is for sorrow   two for joy
three for disappointment   four to meet your boy

can't read their meaning
or that of the storms
rough surf   pounding the shore

swoosh   heard   as a child
in a conch shell   waves
tumbling over and over

flup   flick of the towel
shaking out the sand
before heading back

young Japanese woman
came to Cairns
worked as a diving guide
family's request
her ashes be scattered
on the Great Barrier Reef

her desire was to swim
over delicate coral
as fish
glide
through cold currents
rippling weeds

raped
murdered
her body dumped
in a wheelie bin
put out like garbage
in a swamp

tourists in the sun
gaze upon blue water
sparkles in the brilliance
stirred by a breath of wind
fragile waves tease the shore
weary cameras hang limp

heroine

Vicki Viidikas (1948-1998)

        exotic traveller   in distant places
you are my heroine   mood changer
a look   can make my blood sing   or
bring on the darkness   take my arm
        I walk tall
            until I grow wary

        White Lady   always the stronger lover
exhausted   I crawl ashore   *I'm too frail*
to hold you in my arms   you said
waves crash on rocks   you cannot breathe
caught in a rip   drowning at the reef
        lost   in the change of tides
            I cannot cry my tears

tapping at a typewriter   slight body in the sunshine
drinking *chai*   from cracked rose china teacup

in backyard gardens   down the park   talking baby clothes
laughing future   new man   new book

we no longer sit at smoky meetings   with message of hope
or in a bus stop   sheltering from rain
I   grateful for company   you for the smokes and a meal

doctors want the body   when the baby dies   for science
White Lady powder eases pain   and booze in brown paper bags
pancake flat on my couch   bent spoons in the kitchen

implacable   smoking   coughing   waving hands
in furious gestures   you make me feel important
that I am one of the few who really understand

travelling poor is difficult   drug poems are confused
the respectable withdraw   *all writing is fiction*   you snarl
retreat to rented rooms   neighbours dealing

communal washing machine   filled with dirty syringes
dead people for company

our house in Stanley Street   was a rector's cottage
the old church became The Stanley Palmer Culture Palace
blocks of sandstone and convict brick
sitting back from the road   with a concrete front lawn
broken brick fence   part of the Compound squats
housing hundreds   stretching from Palmer Street to Bourke

I lived there   out the back   seven years in a shed
that once stored grain   now   split level
with a timber floor   and a ladder to my loft
I heard a politician   called us squatters
Urban Blight   when *The Eyes*
sang in Palmer Street   we drank   drugged
danced   some died   then the DMR
came to pull our houses down
create the new highway

a boy lived next door   from when he was twelve
went to prison for possession   raped
wasn't going back   sentenced again for dealing
took an overdose   was dead at 21
Smack Sally   the Dealer   sold drugs for years
kept you waiting   just for fun
as her dog lay at her feet in adoration
not a safe injecting house
kindly sharing needles with friends
they all became infected

Junkie Jo aged 27   going home   packed a few clothes
$7.00 in her pocket   one last taste   she was gone
Hare Krishna devotee   chanted   burnt incense
sent Jo's spirit on its way   body of evidence

cleaned up well before the cops came
I'm charged with cultivation
given a lecture and a good behaviour bond
(police found three small plants)
on TV crops of million dollar plantations

the Dealer wasn't home   when Poet comes to score
'Dapples' the doorbell-dog barks   bites her on the foot
Ginger screams from the top of the stairs
Go away I'm busy   (she sells leaf but doesn't smoke)
Princess in an ivory tower!   mutters the Poet
Waving from the balcony
Won't mix it with commoners   leaves in disgust

Sylvie and I would meet and argue
in the public bar each day
she sitting proud   in neat pink or blues
permed hair stiff with spray
waiting for the boyfriend from the bakery
dramas keeping boredom at bay
swallowed pills with booze
in her room above Beppi's Restaurant
wasn't found for weeks

leaky roof   rain soaked bed   floors awash
our wiring on extension cords
then fires   some lost everything
lost lovers   family   dignity   me too
coughing   shakes   need another drink

where we were   there's a tollway
an air stack above the tunnel   and a sign
change given

waking from a dreaming state is it
stumbling free from drunken men for it
I did not see until my eyes were opened to it

they were loud and violent then because of it
I had thought them friends when out of it
waking from a dreaming state is it

soaking up drunken tales in it
I thought this art with billowing sails before it
I did not see until my eyes were opened to it

bruises   broken bones   and jail in it
hard ground   when tearful fell on it
waking from a dreaming state is it

sullen denial was my fate in it
the way was down   down   down   in it
I did not see until my eyes were opened to it

I do not drink   my choice   is pledged for it
serene   almost   my life is saved by it
waking from a dreaming state is it

I did not see until my eyes were opened to it

girls in our town

the city closed its doors and windows against cold insistent rain

haven't a care
keep asking
they probably will

Julie   unconscious   head bopping up and down   is piggy-backed
in the rain by local boys to hospital   she has a fractured skull
collarbone jaw and missing teeth   the boys jogged Julie down
to save on ambulance fees   she is unemployed and sixteen
next day   the boys come early with chocolates   flowers
cheerful but sheepish grins   let her know   Romeo
is real sorry   can't hold his booze   shouldna' mixed it
with drugs   her eyes are swollen black with the bruising

some leave school at 15

Pus   performance poet   hair the colour of cochineal red/pink shocking
with black roots   punk pretty frock fastened with safety pins
scuffed boots   screeches into a microphone   *'Fuck You Fuck You*
Can you'se hear that?'   more imaginative than   *'Testing One Two Three'*
Pus is performing on a lesbian writers' night at Gleebooks
for Valentine's Day   growling out   grinding bones gnashing teeth
love poems   driving home her exultation's   too traumatic
for a polite audience?   *'Well Fuck You That's It'*   takes a bow
laughs at applause from fresh faced university women   who giggle

her lover is also pleased with her performance
last night Pus won an award   'Most Improved Player'
for extended play with Vixen   who's very skilful
Vixen has many girls on the go   'Most Improved Player'!
this is what being young is all about   experimentation
trust   mixed with danger   smell of leather   stale perfume
whips of pleasure   words of pain   sweet really

so lonely

sudden clap of thunder   sky changes colour   another storm arrives
sheets of rain to bed down the city into darkness

getting old

Kat is homeless   escaping the deluge   huddled in a doorway
Kat believes she is a cat   hair two toned   blonde black
with little peaks   where a cat's ears would be
wears lots of silver   pierced ears nose and lip
torn tartan frock   her T-shirt slogan SEX PISTOLS RULE
covers stained Union Jack   yellow-black striped leggings
suggest feral cat   a red lipstick heart smeared on her cheek
she travels with a friend   his dirty T-shirt bleeds YUPPIES SUK
they've a little carrying case   where two rats reside
the rats are called 'cunt' and 'slut'
people can get quite upset when she's talking to her pets

things might get better

splinters of rain attack the hospital windows   Julie fiddles with a radio
Pus below is a lone figure   bent against the wind   hoping for a lift
worrying   *'where's Vixen tonight?'*   and   *'who's she with?'*
behind the hospital   Kat jumps oily puddles   sloshing her way
to the Church-run soup kitchen   Julie hears on the radio
'No dole payments for those under eighteen'   and bursts into tears
'Weather forecast   heavy rain   easing to showers'
she'll find out next month   she's pregnant

A woman I know
outed herself
to her cat
I'm a lesbian
licking a silken paw
the cat
continued washing
she whispered
You're gorgeous
and gave herself
a pat

Angel and The Butch Balladeer

In feral poets' café   territorial women measure newcomers
grab each other with kisses   I'm drinking *chai*
invited to read my poems   re-edited again and again

Angel slouches against the wall   blonde hair straggly
akubra drawn low   scarf on hips with flat waist
silver ring in navel   torn cargo pants   smoking a thin rolly
improvises: *world spins door opens shuts   Destiny*

Butch Balladeer smiles   denim jacket   blue jeans
tunes a blues guitar: *no singing in the courtroom*
lady   this is serious business
fools can play with sorrow   get caught in the crossfire

Angel smells of sweat   tobacco   patchouli   plays cute
wings it: *hits you in the ovaries   darling   Destiny*

Angel and The Butch Balladeer laugh   hand slap *give me five* salute
grin   share gum   a private joke   and talk through my reading
I see Angel's arm around the Butch Balladeer   so casual

 their eyes devour   hot   salty
 wrapped in torn sheets   cum juice
 fluttering wings   legs flying wide open
 crushed laughter   on the breath
 fresh words   poetry

 they invented sex   this afternoon

k.d.lang: *it's sexy to sit in a suit with shoulders back and legs apart*
Butch is diesel-disco   women who want to be trucks
leather trousers loosened tie   jacket worn just off the shoulder
braces   cropped hair   earring   nose ring   navel
gruff   puff-tough   swagger   with laconic grin
never read a book look
swill swirl the scotch sigh
Butch is charm with a scar
Butch is *stereotype*

Lipstick lez let loose in
frock with flounce   *bold and beautiful* hair
gentle kind frail with giggles
designer grunge or gothic
visible bra   nipple ring and tat
you know what they say
butch on the streets
femme in the sheets

does a soul have gender?
do we paint in only shades of pink
and blue   or slap it on
in all the rainbow hues

Cameron Mahoney (1970-1998)

young man in Ward 17   dying   told it like it is   at eighteen
diagnosed HIV positive   will his father come   does it matter now
never understood   the need for frocks   music that was *just noise*
getting out of it drugs   sleaze balls   Mardi Gras dressed tall
walk the dog   a 12 foot poodle in red tulle

Mardi Gras   what were you doing in '78?
I was so out of it   didn't know it was on   marched the next year
hidden behind a butterfly mask   waiting for cops to attack

in '78 at the Cricketers Arms   every night is party night
beautiful barmen on the bar sing loud: *you'll never walk alone*
glitter queens   flirt with lovers   sparkle nite glamour dramas
I write poems   too many   broken hearts   drugs   booze
on a three day pub crawl   lost my barmaid lover   down at the Rocks
with a Koori woman   smoke   from her didgeridoo bong
disco nights at Red Ruby's   women's music in the Sussex
until I'm barred from both   adrift in a Bob Dylan daze
sunk into shadows of a Joni Mitchell canvas
descend to Darlinghurst squats   days of dereliction   no flags to wave
bruises the colour of rainbows   not invited to party

years later   to be home   drinking tea
watch the parade   listen to them   botch the commentary
crowds cheer   buffed glitter bodies shimmer   *Out There Proud*
marching in support of sons and daughters   dad and mum are on TV
rockets whistle   fireworks   remember friends who've passed
some walk alone

Dr James Walker (1948-1993)

in a photo I have of Jim   he sits on a chair at my window
reading a book on co-dependency   he taught me
freedom of thought   passion for justice   joy
wrapped around me like patchwork quilt   cobbled together
colourful yarns   bit and pieces of the life we knew
as teenagers going to meetings to legalize homosexuality
a 'disease'   a 'crime on the books'   amazed to be Out
flagons of red wine parties   gossip   young men
was it *Maat*   a Goddess to give protection?
he daubed on the walls of my Darlinghurst squat
land rights for gay whales   (that I didn't like
thought a desecration of my space) Jim walked away
would give no more   I was ill with boozing
a disease not a moral weakness?   he could no longer watch

who was it painted his surgery with ugly slogans
gay hate crimes   shaming   blaming him
names of dishonour on his walls at work   *dirty fag*
he went to Egypt   deciphering hieroglyphics
what diseases killed the ancient people
what treatment did their doctors give
we met again   he told me of Isis and Horus
deities and demons   rites of passage
on death and of resurrection
working on another degree   all the time
the virus like lime into porous walls was slowly killing him
I did not watch Jim die   afraid   at the loss of a friend
he faced death and I stayed away
made my excuses   *I've a cold   don't want to give you germs*

watching Mardi Gras
censored for TV
where are sexy sodomy sluts?
time has changed the march
to camera smiles
sparkle for sale
creating empires for other causes
the glitter game is going broke

her aged face   unfamiliar
insurance ad on TV
two years we lived together
twenty years ago
hot sweaty sex
and a man carries her
on his cock around our kitchen
away to a baby in suburbia

middle age is sexy
they're debating on TV
Paul asserts his back
goes out more often
than he does

switch off power
too tired / old
go to bed
my back again

so exhausting
digging deep
exhuming corpses
hurts to make us real
sufferings   get us feeling
turned on the spit
prodded   paraded
self-basted
devouring our own flesh
let go   live & let live
I'm mouthing clichés
in stale smoky air
mirrored secrets
unlocking childhood rooms
stripped away self esteem
cowed by lashings
blame inscribing skin
in glowering silence
an uneaten meal
breathing shallow
remembering
restless shaming
cannot sit with
sifting   shifting
territories of mind

leave for anonymity of a club
faded familiar carpet
cigarette smoke fug
bells ring   coins drop
solitary   lost   again
in the crowd

her voice   stark yellow flowers in cerulean blue
aerial turns on a sunlit stage tethered to a clothesline
wooden peg spinning off   releases shoulder sleeve
round and round in red dust drags the hem
torn on rusty hook   jagged gash in pretty frock

some forty years ago   cleaning bedpans
watching sick children die   I escape
in The Troubadour   hear Jeannie Lewis sing
featherless flight   taking back with me   comfort
through the years   playing scratched vinyl

a voice ethereal   relationships die   people too
on CD   in pubs   theatres   churches
and in my empty sky   I hear her sing
life is for living   we're all dragged in the dirt
wear your scars with pride   crazy melodies

in a city of jewels   she sparkles   beneath white sails
floats   on the rising tide   breathless
husky   from too many cigarettes
years spent in smoky venues   indomitable
her voice soaring to the gods   *till time brings change*

from the West come
flocks of starved birds
bound feet
    tied with ribbon

from Eastern Europe
troupe of Romanian athletes
flying over ruins
    leap into life

suspended in air   a man pounces
women swing / tumble / twirl
percussive beat propels
    tossed bodies into flight

tinkling bells   measure high kicks
move together   spinning handstands
free
    in blue frocks and bare feet

no freedom without discipline
grace without humility
balance without strength
    no joy without dignity

Alibi

from program notes: *creating raw, subterranean*
energy, asking hard, complex questions, and then
letting the pages and photos fall where they may.
– The Dancer Inside

critics savaged the dance performance
Meg Stuart's Damaged Goods   *Alibi*
Festival of Sydney Town Hall production
all on the surface   superficial
the landscape is Rimbaud's
Artaud's *Theatre of Cruelty*
Henke's *Offending the Audience*
this is Colin Wilson's *The Outsider*
one critic wrote   *they are just pretending*

lives of ordinary people
we pass them on the street
the homeless   mad
those that sit asking for help
with a cardboard sign *GIVE ME*
this isn't *Aeros*   where buffed
beautiful athletes   bounce for joy
people beg for attention   are rejected
beaten   they self-harm

pummelling isn't pretty
we stare at them   they scrutinize themselves
wrestle with their demons
hurtle toward familiar violence
war or protest   found on our screens
popular reality TV   it's the local news
reality that has become a spectacle

in the Town Hall's new bare walled asylum
(grimness morphed into a concrete bunker)
we are harangued   the audience laugh
look away   leave noisily   eighty-nine

left one night   fifty-three   I counted
safely exit   counting   this my defence
at seventy-five bucks a ticket
weighing the cost   (I won my seats)

casual acts of violence
confronting loneliness   fractured despair
performers stop   think
numbers click down   clock's running out
they begin again   hurl themselves
in a cold embrace   into the fight
I did it my way   spoken ingenuously
as if we've never heard before
I look at my watch   no interval

this woman will do anything for your attention
cut off a breast   get it enlarged
if you don't want children I'll get my uterus removed
do anything   just so long as you like her
an anonymous man   is so ordinary
it's not me   it just looks like it
walking through a city   he is soon forgotten
another is guilty   of everything
he is powerless   guilty because he cannot fix
what he cannot control

each night   ground into submission
taking a beating   then getting back up
to fall again   to rise and fall
hanging on   tear at faces
combat each other   annihilate themselves
distorting masks of horror
flailing limbs   falling into spasm
<u>I didn't look away</u>

I saw their pain   and mine
I remember beatings   broken bones

golden showers raining down
my murky luck   a hate crime
waking from a coma to live again
I am hollow

time to get back to my feet
trust again   to saunter free
this my alibi?
having got your attention
why am I afraid?

bodies shake   and shake
shake for twenty minutes
Sydney performance poet/dancer
with his partner   join in the trembling
on their seats   their bodies quiver
in an unrelenting cacophony
a young man's torment
his shattering cry
I am glass

I'm wishing all this would end
he's breaking my heart
my friend   whispers
bruising my arm
she holds so tightly

in Tibet   where monks are murdered   you could get shot
listening to the Dalai Lama's words   keeping his photo
or meditating upon his teaching   a taxi driver from Shanghai
is lost   getting from Balmain to Harris Street   uses a map
smiles   when I tell him   I'm going to hear the Dalai Lama
when I arrive   clutching my Ticketek
a volunteer earnestly enquires
What would you ask his Holiness if you could ask one question?
but my mind is blank   *the inside of emptiness*
friend said she'd ask   *When will society be ready for female Lamas?*
I seek a peaceful life   a way of overcoming anger and resentment
having acceptance of death   I sit next to a woman
with a heavy cold   tissues and bottled water
and a man with fruity chest cough
to hear a lesson on the 4 noble truths
the Dalai Lama also has bottled water
for the journey ahead   it's thirsty work
the *cessation of affliction*   from *attachment   anger and delusion*
he ties his shoe laces   his second pair   I heard on the news
he found his only pair of shoes were made in China
I sit worrying   restless   I'll get germs
spread by snuffles to the left   and splutters to the right
I'm fidgety   suck on cough lollies   and worry
on the true path   karma is action   they said no photos
I disobey   sneak a quick one   of a living Buddha

I don't keep my focus   look at the colour of clothes
wanting to be entertained   not to work
this teaching requires   concentration and commitment
the Dalai Lama advises Westerners
stick with your own traditions
the goal is happiness   smiling into the crowd
you need to study further

I leave   desiring fast food takeaway   bought fake Indian food
dried cardboard chicken   burnt *naan* bread with limp lettuce
cessation of suffering   comes when you   *dispel doubts   lingering thoughts*
I go to Paddy's Market   search for a new outfit for a reading
(a piece about my father   an unholy man on the drink)
select a Chinese black peasant jacket-shirt   wonder why later
I'm unhappy   I've a *divine* cold   feel miserable   worrying
must clear the head   wipe away   *attachment*
things that cling   like thick phlegm   dripping nose
an expensive black jacket hanging in the wardrobe

nice to have a hobby
something to share with friends
keeps you out of mischief
I mentioned writing poetry
I cycle   he said   *out over Bondi*
down the coast   Coogee   Bronte
bunch of us get together
have lots of fun
he rides a bicycle
I pedal poetry
wheels on fire
round and round
head miles
on my exercise bike
going places
young and easy in Wales
wandering lonely as clouds
men & women merely players
years lost   babbling
about a black shoe
my soul has swum rivers
recited Oscar Wilde's *The Ballad of Reading Gaol*
to a stationary double decker bus driver
parked just so he could listen
found the beat again
spinning past
tin can box-car locomotives
got off in Sydney
yelling in The Harold Park Hotel
joined the Poets Union
found <u>my</u> voice
one day may win the Poetry Sprint
become a champ

Dorothy Hewett (1923-2002)

was it bats
trapped in dusty corners
flapping black wings
mad mothers screeching
all that family
caused you to flee
no ivory towers
yet a damsel in distress
cascading hair   shaken free
searching through words
rage for warmth
taking shelter
in cinema dream castles
white glove   abandoned on the stair

coming down to earth
in wheat fields   *bobbin'*
spinning yarns
strikes and union men
child's death   hard time's madness
city life   third husband's book
up among tinned food
on a grocery shelf in Darlinghurst
a move to mountains blue
shrieking birds   flash of green feathers
in foggy early morning light
hatred of growing old
under billowing purple velvet skirt
music   still stinging like wasps

mistress of history   a brilliant tactician
wins all the battles   playing by her own rules
with no boundaries   calls the shots
strips bare   innocence
her school girl lover   a child in boxed blue tunic
blonde hair falling   under dark skies
no moon to reveal secrets
gone the taste of oranges
juice spilling down the chin
melted candles leave frozen puddles
on the dresser by the hotel bed
grey waxen tears   gather dust

screen flickerings   deconstruct the river's flow
troops in a dust storm   grey smudges
tanks invading   polished black boots on parade
march to the tune of conquerors
I retreat   flee the city   unable to speak
coward   dishonour in silence
find earth cracking   baked by the sun
huge yellow sunflowers   basking in the glare
when the magic's gone   what is left?
tricks of memory   no blue ice cream
food stains on clothes   absence
burning candles   smell of molten wax

Ubaka is beating her drum
in a small Lilyfield community hall
in my memory   grown there
seeded from song
Ubaka   is singing the world awake
she is healing the earth   cleansing the waters
Ubaka is chanting
we won't fight your war / we won't fight your war
Calling Peace   Calling Peace

Ubaka is beating her beloved drum
magic thrums the air
as women dance   shake their booty
bums and bellies undulate
women stomp their feet
bang the beat on drums
we are shouting
we won't fight your war / we won't fight your war
Calling Peace   Calling Peace

just don't talk to me of war:
crusades against the Infidel   Satan and the Axis of Evil
homicidal dictator   addicted to weapons of mass destruction
the smoking gun that could come in the form of a mushroom cloud

I'm suffering battle fatigue
bludgeoned by speech writers
who never learn their history

don't tell me:
those towel-heads   should pack up their carpets
and go back home to the desert

queue jumpers are illegal refugees   and
you gotta draw the line somewhere don'cha

'Voice of God' voice-over tells me: *warfare isn't natural*
Pyramids of Caral   'Mother City of Civilisation'   in Peru
trading with neighbours   prospers in peace
for a thousand years
the desert blooms   irrigated for cotton
no fortifications   no weapons of battle

commerce not conquest
let's end the slaughter   with another beginning?

On Viewing Russian Ark *at The Valhalla in Glebe*

the film is one grand ninety minutes take
through the centuries   spinning from room to room
fragments of Russian history and art

History is seen loitering in the Hermitage Museum
St Petersburg   evading spies   gasping at beauty in ruins
debating failure of scripture to prepare for the future

orchestras play   dancing lovers in costume drama
indulge in political intrigue   admire lavish table settings
(gold and a blue to die for)   the work of The Old Masters

judged by a blind angel   as cherubs smile
(sniff the pungent odour of the oil)
the Tsar is collecting Art as workers wait for bread

pursued by demons   Catherine the Great
is running through snow
we race after her   breathing difficult

in the cold air   ghostly presence
our unblinking eye   Alexandra
rushing down a corridor trailing servants

exhorts Anastasia not to run
Are we being followed?   Is that a shot?
do we all go to our deaths with the dead watching?

thousands quietly leave   down an ornate staircase
going gracefully to their doom
lost to the way of what was missing

as I exit from The Valhalla Theatre
a musky smell lingers
out on Glebe Point Road   people chat in sunshine

invitations keep arriving   *performances and poetry in the garden of delight*
bring your own or someone else's poetry song story to sing recite chant or
          mumble
bring your favourite cake   (large)   to share with the community....

I'm no writer of pretty garden views   blooming roses   autumnal hues
I see aphids and rust   rain speckles on cracker brown leaves
serpents in the garden of delight   there's no blue dog barking
on a hessian mat   under the lemon tree   behind a grey paling fence
of a city lane way   I've given up on community committee meetings
recycled unbleached minutes   permaculting snobbery that scans
chanting's okay but only for a minute or two   I'm a feral cat
whistling Looney Toons   ready to scratch   not for me
drumming beat of storytellers' magic   lost in the bush   meditating
in crystal thought fields   tea leaf readings using reverse speech
workshops on the power of scent   angel guides to rebirthing
no anxious pull and push of self promotion   working
a tofu mung bean room   tossed salad garden get-to-together
I cultivate   occasional peace of mind   mulching garbage
          yanking weeds

take a lamington says Bernadette   *Sky from Byron will be waiting*
she'll adore your poems   give you nutritional banquets   make love all night
compost your scraps   make organic rainbow dreams come true

I want to be them
I saw Def Poetry Jam at the Sydney Metro
I want to be them
strut and spit and shout
spell passion anger out
buckshot doubt
I want to be them
I want to be   *Colored*   Hispanic
Jam-ai-caaaan   Chinese   Arab
a Nuyorc American
young   gifted   and black
I want to be them
I'm comfortably upholstered
middle aged   no partner   no kids
whitebread bitch
unkool   Aussie dyke
I want to be them

this is not an incantation
no call to prayers   for poetry
but I do ask when word performers
will be recognised
as valuable   as engaged
as any poet on the page
poets performing   be paid
the same respect
to earn a wage
as those that toil upon the page
artistry is bastardry
in wasted time   the guilt is mine
penning words for pleasure
when all I see of Victory
is on a battlefield   in the Sports Arena

I want words to yell at Cardinal Pell
not polite words of regret
published in the paper
what the hell?   George Pell
I'm no *abomination*
a walking stick   my metronome
measures out the rhythm
ears to the wall   my Housing Commission prison
neighbours fight   *fuck you   cunt*   they bellow
I'm dong fine   difficult to define
finding the line   getting the rhyme
creating music of mayhem   making it mine

I'm not a proper performance poet
I don't memorise   extemporise
plagiarise
(well   not often and when I do
I apologise)
I'm too old to talk the jive   hip-hop   rap
but I want to be them
Def Poetry Jammers
I want to be them
I want to sting the heart of a butterfly
I want words to make you cry
I'm doing fine
with the menace   dancing
in the underbelly of the poetry slam
in the black market of our culture
poetry
but when do the words
traded as insults
become   a celebration
of revolution
when are words
a celebration
when
revolution

you leave the safety of your room   going to Tempe's
chimney stacked Pacific Highway wasteland
and a little pub   The Harp   nestled between
takeaway food outlets and industrial projects
a detective   you'd traced the pub in the Metro
asked for the publican to find the Booking Manager
who didn't handle the acts but who put you in touch
with a girl who did but wasn't home
though her boyfriend was   and he said
he was in the band that knew the guys
you were looking for and yes they're playing tonight

Howard   you haven't seen for thirty years
played King Creon to your Antigone
who died daily in High Schools throughout Queensland
what has life added to you except those lines on your face
and that fat on your stomach   you wonder what he's like now
wait for an hour in King Street for a bus connection
an aboriginal woman begs   *'sister,   spare some change,   sister'?*
a man outside the Dendy plays a piano accordion
an Irish military jig   woman in black T Shirt with No War
splattered in blood red pushes past a poster advertising
return of *Hair* to the Capitol   The National Theatre
of Greece is doing Sophocles' *Antigone* at the State....
yours was   Anouilh's   you wonder   get a taxi?

   Poets across the world   have organized a day of protest
   are presenting 10,000 anti war poems to the White House
   UK poems will go to Downing Street   Australian poems
   to Prime Minister Howard in Canberra

you doubt he'll read them   no poetry in him except a passion
for economics   you've watched him on TV
gleeful smile filling the screen   greeting voters
dismissing protesters as   *the mob*

you are late to the gig   Howard   (not the Mr Howard politician)
and his son (conceived on the tour)   are just finishing their set
the young man   blonde and thin   like his mother
(now disappeared from the scene)   plays a mean mouth organ
Howard is trim   gray hair   a conspiratorial grin   looks you over
you wore white jeans back then   now faded black   over the belt flab spills
a girl singing   playing guitar   does a rap poem   about the war
<u>We</u> <u>A</u>re <u>R</u>esponsible   *spells* **WAR**   of Arabic heritage
young and fearless   with a beautiful smile   *this one's for you*
a love song   a rock band is next with vocals that bellow and keen
as the bass guitar screams   you explore the pub
old things stacked on display   an iron pram penny-farthing cycle
typewriter   beer signs   photos of Irish pubs and poets
the young woman who was out when you rang   sings songs
she busked in the streets   lyrics of loss and love
beaming at her friends   girls dance a jig   young kids
adventures yet to live and dreams to lose
gather for a group photo as if they know it will never be like this again

you talk too much about you   nervous   with unraveling memories
old friends   *you don't know what happened   where she is now   is he dead?*
ramble on in the dark   outside the highway is nearly deserted
no more buses   you remember how on tour
school girls thought Antigone an idiot
what would you want to do that for   die   locked away
alive   in a cave just because she put some soil on her brothers corpse
when she shouldna   stop his lost soul wandering around for eternity
Antigone dies to be true to herself   to defeat absurdity of death
by insisting on it   you are no Antigone   burning with idealistic fever
you're tired with swollen ankles   you want to be gathered up
little kid at the end of a party and dropped home
you leave juggling finances for a taxi
you always were intense   Howard says before you part
returning to your room and a screen with the latest news from the BBC

a woman at the Belvoir Street Theatre's *conversations with the dead*
Richard Frankland's play   (investigations into deaths in custody)
black survivor   member of the stolen generation   worries
can she hold on   not leave too soon   before the story ends
shudders   bruises on black skin   being dragged away
taken as a child   carries photos in her purse of the Home
black and white shiny pictures   evidence

small band play guitars   a woman croons
free performance mix   Unwaged and the Industry
the audience look about   comment on the set   *crappy place*
are restless   talk of absent friends   cheer the band   *go bro'*
some are here to coolly appraise the work

harsh truth takes control of the words
anguish shouts   screams through the wall
knives in open wounds slice down to the bone
hung himself with his socks   when he always went barefoot
stabbed himself in his eye with his paintbrush
cut me brother   let the demons out

black actors play white guests at a cocktail party
whine glass elegance   *are you a real aborigine?*

a black diamond snake slithers across tracks in the dust
sacred ground   red earth bleeding
drying rivers weep salty tears
wind curls in blue smoke   long grasses whisper spirit talk

down the hill at Central   sitting on a brick wall
as lights change to red   five homeless men and two women
share bottles of sting   another aboriginal

standing firm on the land   outside her office building
smokes   exchanges small talk   stubs out the butt
yawns   glides back into the glass and steel building
the woman in the theatre   gathering her purse
smiling through tears   remarks to a friend   *good play*

the Industry: people from theatre & the media
sting: coke laced with metho

an old woman at the wharf   spider waiting
as I feared   snags me in her web   *hot isn't it?*
even with the cool sea breeze   *got to get out don'cha?*
I'm going to the Petersham club   Bingo!
may win me a packet of biscuits
"not much of a prize – biscuits"
something for nothing   they'll have me up dancing
but I'm too old for that   I like better to watch
they'll get the Monte-Carlo – "more biscuits?"
no   you take a number   if it's yours well you're out
the last one left   wins
kind to me at the club they were when I fell
they sent for a ambulance but I wouldn't go
they put on stick-on stitches   gave me fifty dollars for a taxi
"better than you sue for thousands"
so I had to join the club   least I could do....
everybody pays their dues sometime

I sit   laugh   savouring a truth
the reason to be alive is to enjoy it – Rita Mae Brown
my neighbour opposite   mutters with hostile intent
oh shut up! not for the first time
while I am otherwise occupied
I hear her mutter   *shut up!*   as if my being alive
is such an imposition   *oh get a life!*   she says
the stationary stalker   watching TV   loudly
three feet away   with the door open   daily
does not move   except to get beer from the fridge
I seek astro advice from the net
being at a loose end isn't the same as being free

come out here!   I'll knock your bloody block off!
screams another drunk neighbour
on my doorstep   after request
not to have TV full blast at 2am
or use the washing machine before 7am
you are a control freak   she curses   *bitch*
trying to run the place
we maintain a frosty silence   resentment
tightens the lips   gets in the way of abundant living

on the road to Gulgong   the bridge is out
take the detour   a dusty unpaved road
in burnished glow through tinted glass of the bus window
cold travellers on a bumpy ride   returning home
snuggle together   in woolly jumpers and trackie pants
talk of the drought   bushfires   floods to come
don't see the landscape artists make into masterpieces
the settlements in long flat plains dotted with rock mountains
grazing sheep and cattle   curious llamas   ignore kangaroo
wombat road-kill   sacrificial offerings   bloodied and abandoned

I'm a finalist at the Festival   in Gulgong   to read one poem
an outsider   at the Ten Dollar Motel   observing
dog-leg streets meander through the old town
pubs with pole verandas horse troughs   a general store
'snap' go whip crackers   horse and carriage promenade
in the grand parade   townsfolk dressed to thrill
bosomy girls swan about   feathers in their hats
outside The Prince of Wales Opera House on Mayne Street
grinning into lens of the local paper   a small boy
on a vintage bicycle   poses in knee britches and cap

mothers with cameras beam   country rhythms percolate
scrubbed boys are winning prizes writing poems
        in the packed Henry Lawson Hall
        a girl in school uniform stands proud
        reads her essay right out loud
        a badge upon her blazer tells it all
        the girl from Gulgong
        wins the Simpson Prize
        travels to Turkey
        to see the sun rise

a tourist   exploring   I search for *faces in the street*
think of Henry Lawson perhaps walking by
long ago thin   sickly   making notes for poems
mooch my way down to the Pioneers' Museum
see Cobb & Co coaches   the blacksmith shop
in yellowing newspapers   local history
among collections of farm machinery
I read about a little boy who ate rat poison
took three days for a doctor to come by horse
but the boy had taken a fit and died

     Lawson was born on the goldfields
     at nine had an ear infection   by fourteen   he's deaf
     an apprentice coach painter   with shearers   a rouseabout
     a loner down on his luck   writing for *The Bulletin*
     on the track   while the billy boils   send round the hat
     in love with Mary Gilmore   (who didn't want to marry)
     wed Bertha   had kids   failed to pay maintenance   inebriate
     went to gaol   to Darlinghurst   going mad   he's locked away
     Henry died at fifty-five   in his sleep   his writing on the bed
     instead of pauper's grave   a magnificent state funeral

I've been a vagabond in drink
lost in locked wards   not allowed to leave
I limp with a stick from an old injury
know how it feels to be broke   lonely
walking the streets without hope
I heard a tale of a 'lady's waist'
left on the bar in pubs on William Street
Henry's glass   each and every one left
half full   publicans would say 'don't touch …
that's Henry's glass …'

I'm assured acoustics are perfect in the Gulgong Royal Opera House
where Melba once sang   no need for a microphone
more than nervous   in blinding lights
expected to be 'intimate'   'with a voice of the modern Lawson'

as the audience imbibe local wine   poetry and a theatre piece
consumed with a meal of roast chicken or beef
friends meet again to hear stories judged the best
to lucky winners   prize money and a statuette of Henry
laughter and applause welcome my words   a stranger from the city
a long way to travel   down country roads   so far from home

Faces in the Street, July 1888
In the Days When the World was Wide and Other Verses, Henry Lawson
lady's waist: small glass (7 ounce)

into the city   on the back of a ute   come fibreglass cows
Picowsso   Mootilda (Queen of the Desert)   *Cudding Edge*
Cowpaccina (a cafe cow)   *Great Barrier Beef*
and his sister *Ally McVeal   Moolin Rouge* stands
struts her stuff at the Queen Victoria building
as the *Queens Cownsell*   red and black player-card queens
(with grey wig)   holds court inside
a brown cow does voice exercises at the Opera House
on a street corner   a mustard yellow black striped udder
with citrus tang cow placidly waits and waits
colours run on wildberry cows outside Customs House
seated in the rain   CashCows queue at ATMs
Cowputer busy number crunching at the Stock Exchange
goofy green St George cow plotting takeovers in Martin Place
at Chifley Square   *Cowmen Miranda*   a fire engine red
banana yellow flowers cow   with wobbly fruit hat
batting eyelashes   is flattered by all the attention
Ken Done cow   crouched chewing cud
on the footpath in front of Qantas   worries
But ... Is it Art?

cattle   stare into spaces   no normal cow could contemplate
skyscrapers   cars stalled in traffic   women in high heels
men in italian suits swishing to work   polluted haste
as busy people   stop   smile   pat cows
tourists pose   friends have their photos taken with
children   jump astride   apricot   jungle green   kingfisher blue
hyacinth and pink   patched cows
there's even an aboriginal one   cobalt blue
with chocolate dot-paintings   down near Bennelong Point

do the cows get up and walk about?
sniff at fine leather coats on display   thinking of lost cousins
view beef patties with distaste at McDonald's
worry about mad cow disease   have recurring nightmares
mounds of slaughtered   burning cattle   at 3am
do they lope across the Harbour Bridge in mOOnlight
stop and stare   at bright lights in tall buildings
peer toward the Smiley Face of Luna Park
watch the Manly Ferry   longing to cruise   wonder
at exotic animal noises (the roar of lions) wafting
across the water from Taronga Zoo
do they go for a drink from the Tank Stream
snooze in Farm Cove   escape for mOOvable feasts
in the Botanical Gardens   lie down in green pasture
cow pats and flies   dream of open space   blue sky   flat horizon

Holy cows!   where are the chains of marigolds?
devotees chanting   drumming
offerings of incense and fodder
there's no respect for happy hoofers
only in Australia   louts
riding rough shod the work of artists
rope 'em   ride 'em   brand 'em
cowboys   *rustle   smash to pieces   breakin' in*
the moo moos
(and what can you do with broken hoofs on a painted plastic cow?)

mOOving on milked the public for sympathy
an *udderly mooving marketing tool*

Charity cows   after mustering
the steers are auctioned off
to the highest bidder
become a collector   buy a ceramic figurine
from a herd of 12 bovines   (released three times a year)
or a better bargain   beanie bag beasts
click for the *international herd*
or visit   www. cowparade.net.au

a dig

careful brushings in the midden
what will be found after 1000 years
shard of pottery   hank of hair
artefacts of the nuclear age
strange metals that travelled
to the moon and back
among weapons of mass destruction
a cricket ball and bat
layers of silt reveal
hub cap   saucepan
plastic drink bottles   a biro
colourful flags of unknown origin
robotic dog   cloned sheep
a bright green feather
lengths of string in a rusty biscuit tin
magazine photos of a major movie star
her muscles flexed for action

nothing is new on the planet
at the end   of the 20th Century
old man's placard
THE END IS NIGH
face of doom
turned to the wall
as he rests
sipping coffee
in Martin Place